UPHEAVALS

ZACKARY LAVOIE

Perpetual thanks to my many mentors throughout the construction of this chapbook and the poems inside of it.

A special thanks to the professors at the University of Maine at Farmington for their amazing work, specifically Jeffrey Thomson, Kristen Case, and Pat O'Donnell.

Another thank you to Alice James Books for allowing me to spend my fall with these poems as their Director's Chair Fellow.

Thank you to Pond Bench Press for allowing me to share my work and giving me so much autonomy with this publication, and Cameron Morrell for the beautiful cover art.

Finally, thank you to Kaveh Akbar, Roy G. Guzmán, Jacques J. Rancourt, Devin Kelly, Chelsea Dingman, and the countless other poets whose love for poetry is so pure it knows no bounds.

Versions of these poems, some under different titles, have appeared in *Empty Mirror Magazine, Dirty Paws Poetry Review, OCCULUM Journal,* on the '*memoria*' Podcast and elsewhere. Boundless thanks to the editors of these publications.

Cover art by Cameron Morrell

Published by Pond Bench Books Inc.

ISBN: 0692052828

ISBN 13: 978-0692052822 (Pond Bench Press Inc.)

for the sleepy boy

TABLE OF CONTENTS

a gentle push of autumn.
violet skies and
indigo hands and
white knuckles.

leaves from a juvenile tree
inevitably brown.

upheaval of rhubarb wisdom

Growing Rhubarb in the back garden.
        Broad, leafy ears resembled my own.
        I can sit and see myself grow between the foxgloves
and snapdragons.

Plant when he's dormant in the fall.
        Harvest in March.

Rhubarb flesh
is wet and firm and   tangy enough.
Barn-red stalks with stringy ligaments
and waxy skin.

A spoonful of sugar under a tongue is sweet. but rhubarb
        broken off at the base and   masticated, is
 especially tart. Too many tastes can be toxic.

My joints are inflamed.

Now,
on a bed of cinnamon and nutmeg,
    lay the morsels evenly and bathe him
in strawberries and splash with vanilla (that's the secret).

Cover with a lattice blanket and tuck him in
        the oven to bake. When he's finished,
serve warm, with cream.

1

rock dove under ditmars (i)

I do not walk underneath the Q train on Ditmars Boulevard.

35th is dank
and dripping with the
unwanted and unlovely.

The Rock Dove keeps to himself,
head down, pecking aimlessly
at refuse lining the pillars of the bridge.

He does not lift his head, but flutters
from one side
of the Avenue to
the other.

I take the train to
30th and walk to Hoyt,
then down 29th
past The Sparrow Tavern,
before I get to 23rd

He huddles into his
corner of the universe--
his nest--
and ruffles his feathers.

Look

Above him and Ditmars,

above car horns and humid buses
is another nest, much larger
than his.

I have to walk up
four flights of stairs
in a five-floor apartment
building. The lights dim
the windows big.

A Peregrine Falcon tilts her head
and looks at the gray skyline,
ablaze with sunset
and jagged like uncut opal.

She stretches her wings
a barrier between the Dove
and the sun.
A menacing eclipse.

rock dove under ditmars (ii)

I do not walk underneath the Q train on Ditmars Boulevard.

She lived
on the floor above me.
Her hair fell
in loose curls over
pale shoulders.

Layered feathers,
glistening bronze, the
air beneath her
talons
hard.

In a graceful dive
she plummets
towards
the wet sidewalk.

My eyes were heavy with the heat of day.
The moment my door closed
I heard feet hurry down
the stairs. Malice in her toes.

Swift as she may be
the Dove begins his
escape, only
to be caught and ruined.

4

The Falcon pinches

her beak and snaps

individual ribs
picking at the meat between them.

She said it
with such force
I wrapped my arms around
my torso to protect myself.

When she is finished
she leaves him
in the street, his body heavy
with heat,
leaning against
the curb.

cognitive dissonance

To repress what lust that sits in my jaw
I will hold it shut.
I will feel bone on bone
Rub and grind and file away.
I will hold my teeth together this
Close.
Each molar will find its partner
And embrace each crevice and curve.

I will not open my mouth,
Not for you.

upheaval of a sad woman

The untailored hive
Still acts
As a penultimate

Dollhouse & inside
Unbraidable nimbleweed
Praying
To an ex-goddess

Hoisted atop
Her pagan tower.
In the applelight
You can see her
Mouthful

Of crosshatched dogteeth.
She is smiling
Because tomorrow
Her oarsmen
Will carry her
To the trestle &

She will jump.
In a plume of out flung petals she will punctuate the cymballed
ritual she has chiseled for herself.

upheaval of a tired man

living in the back of a dying dog's mind   carrying along

whatever else is left   i'm never sure. i try to listen from a
distance.

the brightest part of a candle is in the center of the

flame and i am ablaze. i always thought the short hand on a
clock was more

important than the minute hand because important things
move slowly. my

skin tastes like soil and honey. my father taught me how to tell
hours

until the sun sets by holding my fingers   just so
between the horizon and tangential to the base of

the sharp sphere   but my fingers are too big and i am
always inside before dark.   if i could create

a religion i would pray to trees and call them mother. instead i
play with god

in the morning when he is lonely.
 in the first grade

my teacher gave my parents a questionnaire and now i know i

respond well to positive reinforcement.

sometimes i wonder which horseman of the apocalypse i
embody. usually i am a gentle plague with a three heads.

if god

lives on earth
i'm sure he hangs
onto the underside
of a fallen leaf
that floats on
a small pond
somewhere rainy
and dead
because of its closeness
to the local cemetery
on the banks of a river flooded
so high the steps
that lead into it are already completely
under.
i'm sure he sits
on the singular
step of his porch
and feels the silt
between the cracks
between the bricks
between his toes
and wonders
if the worms
can feel the vibrations
of his thoughts
about locusts and war.
no one here is listening.

early october

i have nightmares in the honeysuckle hour between
sunrise and when you wake   bruises from sleeping
with my legs crossed tightly and my arms under my
armpits   i have been here before
when the coils under me freeze and the bed is hard
i crack the way ice   cracks when it's
dropped in sweet tea

            my fingers dig past your breast and i scratch inside
your ribs   the weeps of women misheld by   shaky hands
are not unfamiliar to me and yours is no different in tone
but the inertia that carries your   sobs and soft beggings pins
me
to the headboard and you feed me chocolate and blueberries
until my mouth bleeds

hooks of dead trees push against
a gray   sky like burrs on a bare foot

this morning i watched a leaf die i watched

the supple life drain from
its stem and saw rust   inhaled from its imperfect edges

i die the same way   from the outside in

my father stands in clarion water

Scarred palms
cast his hand crafted
fly fishing rod into a stream in Oquossoc.

His
arm, like the drink he stands in,
moves in consistent patterns;
he can be predicted and expected,
and like the clouds he stands under,
quiet and looming.
Endless sheets of rain and thunder
in his chest.

When he looks at my mother,
his wife, with an uncompromising,
warm,
stare, the room is hushed,
if only for these few
taut
moments.

Shakes my hand
as though he were applying for
a job I was hiring for.

He sits and waits in the car while I
finish saying goodbye
to a girlfriend I've had for no more than a month.
Helped me buy a $70 dollar ring for her.

And when ring after ring had come
and gone, he remains
there,
in his big, ivory truck.

upheaval of the ideation

there's more than one
way to stop a suicide, you know. the one that works
best is grabbing me
by the back of the arm
the way a father does
before you run into the street,
or the way a girlfriend does
after an argument and she doesn't *actually* want you to leave
yet.

it's been three years now.

even though there is no door, there is still space
to sleep in the dead flora. a drying waterlily
 will keep you company, i think.

 ice on both banks is choking the river.

i spent this morning on the bridge above
comparing bodies to mountains
and how happiness can leave the body through sublimation if
the surrounding air is hot enough.

have you ever noticed how winter sunsets look so far away?

14

take the blood from my willing corpse and boil

the iron from it.
    tell me how
        to admit to my body i no longer
covet it.

dip me in honey and let it harden
so that i might feel the solitude an amber-trapped mosquito
feels.
allow the shallow roots of lichen to take hold of my pores so
that fervent color paints my skin.
let loam support the base of my neck and
satiate the hollows of my collar bone with beechnuts to be
roasted
by hot resonance in my chest.

i am waiting for the river to overflow and fill my belly
with pebbles.

my savior goes by the name *Populus tremuloides.*

he stands and waits
    for the wind to force
        him to act alive in autumn.
inoculate me.

aubade to rest after abuse

Eroded by molten words,
retreat to a state of unawareness.
Breath softens and frustrations leak
from lips onto the sheet.
Eyes flick and swipe at imagined images
as if they were drenched in paint,
each stroke
an impressionist's fuzzy dream.

The occasional stir of evening air tilts the knuckles of the
curtain's folds.
    gossamer breeze
Edges have melted into themselves.
    liquid silhouettes
                There is rest in this place. Droplets from a
                leaky sink
                have gone to sleep. Flowers on printed
                wallpaper
                have gone to sleep. Faces formed by popcorn
                ceilings
                have gone to sleep.

But repose is temporary.

Solitude is fractured
when spears of light
force
        their way
between

16

      drapes.

A fissure
created.

Serene sheets have become tumultuous.
Soft down to waves,
Mounds of polyester to bergs.

Now rise--
        Unbent

upheaval of the attempt as a gun

If He is upstairs His footsteps are quiet. Like a flank of lamb
on a hot stone, I am searing. The hair on the back of my neck

stands and is singed by direct impingement and heat seethes
down
my Picatinny vertebrae. As I lay upon scorched earth, the
nerves, originating

from the base of my hips, become threaded and harden. Here,
looking up
from the base of this tree, the highest branches form an iron
crosshair

pushed hard against the sky's temple. I wonder if you take the
pressure
created by all the hands pressed together in prayer and put it
against

a trigger if it would fire. I wonder if the sound of it going off
would echo
against the nave of the church or of the person. I'm starting
                              to think.
The air here has started to pull me the way an oar pulls
the water around it in vortexual thrusts.
                    Listen:
awareness and disgust have become the same and I am sick.
We are sick.

orr's island, first frost

a cabin hugs harpswell's rocky outline   at the shore a
foamy divide
between chlorophyllic solitude and high tide   movement is
less complicated here
     but it is movement nonetheless

translucent brown glass tumbles
with fog and brine

slapping against slate and tossing into tide pools   their task

refinement

barnacles spot the back of my throat

a temperate taste of
two sugars   nothing else but

undergrown overgrowth

upheaval of blame and a tea party

Now I seize in a clump of dirty sheets.

How many months must a stone lay in the bed of a stream before the stone forgets about the surface? The water is colder than before.

Have you ever seen a Sunflower on a windowsill? If you look close enough, you can

count the seedless pits.

I have always stepped on the acorns that littered the driveway & never thought twice but now

even that has changed.

Sweet rosewater pretends to spill into an empty plastic teacup. I drink it anyway & smile across a table never set for any more than myself.

ferns

the verdant glow that is born
when light reflects on the underside of a new leaf

have you ever heard a brittle branch fall into algae
covered pond water

have you ever listened to a wet pinecone thud against
a tin roof

departures create ripples and those ripples will spread until
they run into something or they become so small they revert
remnants of recurved ridges

the room has been warm since you left

upheaval post attempt

You, rotten saddlebag,
You, thick mercury,
Muted canvas, Deer tick,

Have been detached. Carnation air fills
These deflated left-behinds. I've gotten rid

Of the red handkerchief. Now I cough
Blood into my own hands instead.

I wonder,
Do you still wander under the overpass?

Looking for something to break against
Its graffitied pillars? Maybe

One day you'll throw yourself
Through the concreate

And come out the other side a little less
Of a fist and a little more
Of a cupped hand of milk and caramel.

What home can be made of twine
And still house a hearth?
That wick is nothing but a failed noose suspended in unmelted
Wax.

upheaval of the convalescence

and when the gusts had softened we were
upside down   all we had were the milky stalks of dandelion

our shoestrings lashed like devil tongue

we wanted to bend for something solid the way a
drooping willow gets so close but hardly ever touches
the ground

the moss   oh   the sleepy moss
scrambled for a spot on the moon

the pebbles that made up our walkway became marbles
bouncing against each other and so did we

god song

God once

hooked lines to my waist & bounced me from clouds to mud
                    He spoke

to me through a blade of grass pinched between his thumbs &
                    He told

me to go to the river & soak my tired feet until they no longer
stung
                    He said

feed the ducks   sleep on a bed of ferns   break bread
                    He said

& be fed in return
                    He plucked

leaves from an Oak & put them over my eyes
                    He vibrated

with the hum of a thousand bees

nearer to you
                    He said

nearer to me

Praise

"Rhubarb grows from rhizomes, releasing its body wherever conditions prove favorable. Similarly, Zackary Lavoie's poems in Upheavals contain those rhubarb-like qualities of disruption and alteration, an I that vanishes and reappears in the natural world, in the city, in the sacred, and back in a corporeal body. There is a rich curiosity in Lavoie's poems that reminds me of how Elizabeth Bishop, Matthew Henriksen, Neruda, Blake, and William Carlos Williams devise imagery in their works. "if i could create // a religion i would pray to trees and call them mother," Lavoie claims in world replete with myth, flora, and longing. These poems will meander like rivers to "fill [your] bell[ies] with pebbles," and you won't soon forget their humming."

 -Roy G. Guzmán, author of the forthcoming collection, *Catracho*, from Graywolf Press.

"Zackary Lavoie's Upheavals is a book of transformations, of the failure of the natural and spiritual world to serve as salve: "If god / lives on Earth / i'm sure he hangs / onto the underside / of a fallen leaf … somewhere rainy / and dead." Meditative yet spurred by urgency, these poems contemplate the precipice of despair and desperation, of suicide and escapes. A votive to memory, to the father who stays behind in his ivory truck and to the overpass that spans above these poems, they offer--in spite of lushness--no simple solutions. "the brightest part of a candle is the center of the / flame," Lavoie writes, "and i am ablaze." Heaving, jagged, and sharp, like ice pinnacles, Upheavals pierces with beauty."

 -Jacques Rancourt, author of *Novena*.

(cont.)

"To make of your body a prayer is, I think, one of the humble ways we become holy, and here, in this hymnal full of elegies, Zackary Lavoie has performed such spiritual supplication. These poems are wonder-filled, a child's fingers running through the dirt. They ask what I wish we always asked: how can I become a little smaller? And then they gaze, beg, question, pray, and praise. Sit with these and let them warm your room. Sit with these and count the bruises you acquired in sleep. Sit with these and then leave that room and find the world outside and look, as these poems do, a little closer. Zackary says, "if I could create / a religion i would pray to trees and call them mother." Shh, don't tell him, but in Upheavals, he does just that."

    - Devin Kelly, author of *In This Quiet Church of Night, I Say Amen.*

"Zackary Lavoie's *Upheavals* marks the path of a poet searching for God and grace and human connection in a dead pigeon killed on Ditmars, in a wet pinecone thudding on a tin roof, in a lover's morning departure as the sun spears its bars of light between the drapes. Here is the benediction of loneliness. Here is the architecture of want. Step inside and be transformed. You will "come out the other side a little less/ Of a fist and a little more/ Of a cupped hand of milk and caramel."

    -Jeffrey Thomson, author of *The Belfast Notebooks.*

~

Zack Lavoie graduated from the University of Maine at Farmington and is the author of the chapbook UPHEAVALS (Pond Bench Press). He was awarded the 2017 Alice James Books Director's Chair Fellowship in Farmington, Maine, where he lives. He is a feedback editor at Sooth Swarm Journal, and works as an ESL editor for a global trading platform. His work can be found in Empty Mirror Magazine, OCCULUM Journal, Dirty Paws Poetry Review, on the 'memoria' podcast, and in other beautiful journals.

Made in the USA
Coppell, TX
22 December 2019

13679726R00023